Conversation Starters

for

Charles Belfoure's

The Paris Architect

By dailyBooks

  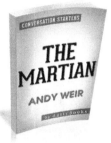

Tips for Using dailyBooks Conversation Starters:

EVERY GOOD BOOK CONTAINS A WORLD FAR DEEPER THAN the surface of its pages. The characters and their world come alive through the words on the pages, yet the characters and its world still live on. Questions herein are designed to bring us beneath the surface of the page and invite us into the world that lives on. These questions can be used to:

- Foster a deeper understanding of the book
- Promote an atmosphere of discussion for groups
- Assist in the study of the book, either individually or corporately
- Explore unseen realms of the book as never seen before

About Us:

THROUGH YEARS OF EXPERIENCE AND FIELD EXPERTISE, from newspaper featured book clubs to local library chapters, *dailyBooks* can bring your book discussion to life. Host your book party as we discuss some of today's most widely read books.

Table of Contents

Introducing *The Paris Architect*

THE PARIS ARCHITECT TAKES PLACE IN FRANCE DURING the Nazi occupation of the country during World War II. The main character of the novel, Lucien Bernard, is an architect. At the beginning of the story, Lucien meets with a wealthy man by the name of AugusteManet. Lucien has been struggling to have food and other necessities during the war, and he is excited to have potential work. However, he soon finds out that the work Auguste wants him to do is dangerous and potentially life-threatening.

Auguste tells Lucien that he wants him to build a secret room. The secret room will hide Mendel Janusky. Mendel is a wealthy, Jewish man who is using his money to help other Jews escape from Europe. This work is challenging for Lucien because he has no sympathy towards the Jews, and is afraid of what will happen to him if the Nazis find out. However, Lucien cannot resist the money that is being offered. Auguste even sets Lucien up with a job building a munitions factory for the Nazis in exchange for his help. Lucien agrees to do the work for Auguste.

Lucien is married to Celeste and having an affair with Adele. Celeste is not pleased with Lucien's decision to work with the Nazis. She is afraid that the French Resistance will attack him if they find out. Adele, however, is having another affair with a Gestapo commander, Colonel Schlegal. Colonel Schlegal calls for Mendel to be found then tortured and interrogated.

Lucien helps hide the Jews initially because he likes the challenge of designing the secret room. He is not concerned about the people until a Jewish couple dies in one of his rooms due to smoke inhalation. Lucien then sees that they are real people who need help and devotes himself to helping the Jews.

Lucien develops a friendship with Major Herzog, a Nazi officer, while working in the munitions factory. Major Herzog helps Lucien with many of his design projects. Meanwhile, Colonel Schlegal has discovered hiding spaces in a mansion. He begins questioning many designers and craftsmen in the area. Lucien takes on Alain as an apprentice. Lucien is unaware, but Alain's uncle is a Nazi.

Eventually, the French Resistance discovers that Lucien is working with the Nazis. In order to prove that he is innocent, the French Resistance makes him blow up one of the munitions factories that he built. Celeste leaves him and never finds out about the other projects he is working on to hide the Jews. Lucien begins an affair with a woman named Bette, who is also hiding Jews, mainly Jewish children. Lucien adopts one of the Jewish orphans, Pierre. Alain finds out that Lucien has been building hiding spaces to help smuggle Jews out of Europe. However, Pierre kills Alain before he can tell anyone Lucien's secret.

Colonel Schlegal finds out that Mendel is hiding in a building near Gestapo headquarters. Colonel Schlegal calls Lucien into the building to help him find where Mendel is hiding inside the building. Lucien tries to stall until Major Herzog gets there. When Major Herzog arrives, he dismisses Colonel Schlegal. He then tells Lucien that he knows about the hiding places. He helps Lucien, Bette, the children, and Mendel escape France.

Introducing the Author

CHARLES BELFOURE WAS BORN IN BALTIMORE, MARYLAND, on February 19, 1954. Belfoure was born to Charles Belfoure, Sr. His mother was the famous writer and a teacher, Kristine Vetulani, who was a Polish immigrant. Belfoure grew up in a suburb of Baltimore, called Woodlawn, where he also attended high school. He is currently residing in Westminster, Maryland.

Following high school, Belfoure attended the Pratt Institute where he studied Architecture and obtained a bachelor's degree in the subject. Following his time at the Pratt Institute, Belfoure attended Columbia University where he obtained a Masters of Science in Real Estate Development. After he had completed his studies, Belfoure went on to teach at the Pratt Institute and Goucher College. He also worked as a writer for *The Baltimore Sun* and *The New York Times*.

Prior to his adult life, Belfoure was not a writer. He realized he enjoyed writing in his late 30s while writing his thesis for his master's degree at Columbia University. He took his love for writing and began writing non-fiction works about architecture. He jokes that he eventually "fooled himself into thinking he could write fiction" as many writers of non-fiction do. He was inspired by John Grisham, who is a lawyer and used his legal background as the inspiration for his stories. He decided to use his background in architecture to inspire his novels.

When editing a story, Belfoure takes a lesson from painting, which he does as a hobby. When he paints a picture, he puts the painting facing a wall and doesn't look at it. After a few months have passed, he decides whether or not it's good as it is, needs revision, or needs to be thrown away. Belfoure uses the same approach when writing. He leaves the story alone for a short period of time. Then, he goes back to it to see what stands out and what needs to be taken out of the story. He also stresses the importance of having someone else read and edit his story honestly, without worrying about his feelings.

Belfoureis known as a specialist in historic preservation. He has been published several times on the topic of architectural history. He has also received a grant from the Graham Foundation to do architectural research.

Discussion Questions

. . . .

question 1

Consider the characterization of Lucien. What, in the novel, is evidence to show why Lucien held beliefs he did toward the Jews at the beginning of the story? Do you think Lucien was anti-Semitic? Why do you think as you do?

. . . .

question 2

At the beginning of the novel, Lucien agrees to build AugusteManet's secret room, despite his apprehensions. Why do you think Lucien chooses to accept the job? What does it say about Lucien's character that he accepted Auguste's job for the reasons he did?

. . . .

question 3

Lucien has a change of heart towards the Jews after he finds out a Jewish
couple has died in one of his rooms. What do you think it was about the
situation that caused Lucien to change his outlook? Why do you think it took
him so long to feel empathy for the Jews?

. . . .

. . . .

question 4

Consider the topics of artistry and skill in *The Paris Architect*. Lucien
mentions that he marries Celeste because she is aesthetically pleasing. It
makes sense to him that an artist should have a beautiful wife. Lucien
considers Major Herzog to be a good person because of his skill and interest
in architecture, even though Major Herzog is a Nazi. What does this say
about the importance of artistic skill in the novel? Is it fair to state that
artistry is considered more than a person's character? Why do you think as
you do?

. . . .

. . . .

question 5

Consider the ending of the novel. Lucien mentions that art is an illusion. Why do you think Lucien feels this way at the end of the novel? What do you think changed his mind about art?

. . . .

. . . .

question 6

Lucien is conflicted when he thinks about Major Herzog. He realizes that he is helping the Nazis by building for them. However, he believes Major Herzog is not as evil as other Nazis because he shares his passion for art. Do you think it is fair to judge a person's character on what they are passionate about? Why do you think as you do? Why do you think Lucien believed Major Herzog to be a good person because of his passion for the arts?

. . . .

question 7

Many of the characters must work for and against the Nazis. AugusteManet
has to work with the Nazis to more effectively help the people he is hiding.
Lucien works for the Nazis for personal gain, but also works against them by
building the hiding places. Do you think these characters are "traitors," as
Celeste said? Why do you think as you do?

· ·

question 8

Lucien has strong feelings about the French Resistance. He believes that the French Resistance killing people only makes it easier for the Germans to massacre large numbers of people. Do you agree with Lucien's position? Why or why not? Why do you think Lucien ultimately decided to support the French Resistance.

· ·

question 9

Consider how the French people think of Jews and how the Nazis think of Jews. Consider the stories of the Serraults and Juliette in particular. How do the two definitions of Jewish people differ?

. . . .

question 10

During World War II, France is largely anti-Semitic. The book makes a
distinction between Jews native to France and Jews born outside of France.
What are some examples in the novel that show this distinction between
foreign-born Jews and French Jews?

. . . .

. . . .

question 11

Many of the French people refuse to help the Jews during World War II. Why
do you think they choose not to help people who are being massacred daily?
What reasons do you think they have for not helping? Are their reasons
valid? Why or why not?

. . . .

· ·

question 12

Throughout the novel, many of the French people would inform one another.
However, there were also people that helped people, such as AugusteManet.
Do you think war brings out the worst in people or the best in people? What
reasons do you have to support your position?

· ·

. . . .

question 13

In the novel, Juliette's husband left her because she was considered Jewish.
What do you think his motivation was for leaving? Can you defend his
actions in any way? Why do you think as you do?

. . . .

. . . .

question 14

Many fictional representations of World War II, including *The Paris Architect*, depict the Nazis as evil monsters. *The Paris Architect* shows the character of Major Herzog, who is a Nazi but also has a compassionate side. Do you think, in reality, that there were Nazis, such as Major Herzog, who despised what they were doing? Why do you think as you do?

. . . .

. . . .

question 15

The Nazis are often portrayed as evil monsters, and historically, there is a lot of evidence to back up this position. For those who did not want to be part of the Nazi party, why do you think they joined the Nazis? Do you think they had a choice? If they just followed the crowd, despite their opposition to what the Nazis were doing, does that make them just as bad as the people, like Colonel Schlagel, who had no conscience while carrying out their acts? Why do you think as you do?

. . . .

· ·

question 16

A few readers were disappointed by the ending of *The Paris Architect*. They felt there should be more suspense as the entire book was suspenseful. Do you agree with these readers? Why do you think as you do?

· ·

. . . .

question 17

A few readers felt as though the historical context was out of place in a few areas. Specifically, they mentioned the passage where Lucien talks about the classic angel on one shoulder and devil on the other scene used in films. Do you agree with these readers that a few passages seemed "out of place" for the period? Why do you think as you do?

. . . .

. . . .

question 18

Many readers felt as though *The Paris Architect* was not the most profound novel, but it was an intriguing story nonetheless. Do you agree with these readers? Why do you think as you do?

. . . .

. . . .

question 19

One reader wrote that Charles Belfoure made Paris in 1942 "come alive" through vivid imagery and descriptive words. Do you agree with this reader? Why do you think as you do?

. . . .

question 20

One reader called Lucien "despicable" at the novel's beginning. The reader could not understand why they would care about a character who seemed heartless. Do you agree with this reader's opinion on Lucien? Why do you think as you do?

  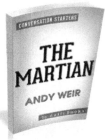

. . . .

question 21

Some readers have taken issue with the amount of swearing that happens in the book. They find it distracting and say it takes away from the story. Do you agree with these readers? Why do you think as you do?

. . . .

. . . .

question 22

One reader felt as though the characters in the novel were not fully developed and lacked motivation for their actions. The reader used the example of Pierre killing Alain to back up their claim. Do you agree with this reader on the character development in the novel? Why do you think as you do?

. . . .

. . . .

question 23

Many readers found AugusteManet, Juliette, and Bette to be their favorite characters. Which characters in the story were your favorites? Why were they your favorites?

. . . .

. . . .

question 24

Many readers commented that there was a large amount of sexism found in
The Paris Architect. One reader gave the example of Lucien charging into
Bette's apartment, resisting the urge to punch her, and ordering her around
her apartment. Do you agree with these readers? Did you find sections of this
book where men were made to seem or acted as though they were more
important than women?

. . . .

. . . .

question 25

One reader wrote in their review that the characterization and transformation of Lucien was "well developed" and "humanly realistic." Do you agree with this reader? Did you like Lucien's transformation and find it realistic? Why do you think as you do?

. . . .

question 26

Charles Belfoure began his writing career by writing non-fiction, and then he transitioned to fiction writing. What do you think about the author's decision to write fiction after writing non-fiction? Do you think non-fiction writing helped him in his fiction writing?

question 27

Charles Belfoure worked as a teacher prior to writing. Do you think his teaching career helped him in his writing career? Why do you think as you do?

. . . .

question 28

Charles Belfoure has an interesting strategy for editing his writing. He does not look at his writing for a period of time, then goes back to it to see what will stay and what should be revised or removed. What do you think of his editing strategy? Do you think it is an effective way to edit?

. . . .

. . . .

question 29

Charles Belfoure was inspired by John Grisham to write fiction novels. Grisham is a lawyer turned novelist. Belfoure began as an architect, then he became a novelist. Both authors use their backgrounds in their novels. What do you think of Belfoure and Grisham using their previous professions in literary works? Do you think it is a good way to approach writing? Why do you think as you do?

. . . .

. . . .

question 30

Charles Belfoure is a hobbyist painter and a historical preservationist in
addition to being an architect and writer. Do you think any of his other
hobbies or jobs help him when it comes to writing? In what ways could they
be helpful?

. . . .

. . . .

question 31

Lucien created many hiding places throughout *The Paris Architect*. If you
were a Jewish person who had to hide during World War II, which hiding
place would you choose and why?

. . . .

. . . .

question 32

In *The Paris Architect*, Lucien accepts work from opposing sides in World War II. He builds hiding places for Jews to be smuggled out of Europe, and he builds munitions factories for the Nazis. How would the story be different if he had not helped build munitions factories? How would the story be different if he had not built the hiding spaces?

. . . .

. . . .

question 33

Lucien's wife, Celeste, leaves Lucien after the French Resistance discovers he is making munitions factories for the Nazis. She is also unhappy when she initially finds out that he is aiding the Nazis. Would you have reacted in the same way as Celeste if you were married to or a close friend of Lucien? What would you have done the same or differently?

. . . .

· ·

question 34

AugusteManey and Mendel Janusky devise a plan to help smuggle Jews out of Europe. If you were living in Europe during World War II, would you have done the same as these people? Would you have helped hide and smuggle Jews out of Europe? Why do you think as you do?

· ·

question 35

Lucien agrees to help build the hiding places to hide Jews even though he was consciously aware it was a dangerous job with great risks. Would you have made the same choice as Lucien even though there was a risk of severe punishment? Why do you think as you do?

. . . .

question 36

Lucien eventually adopts Pierre as his son. How might the story be different
if Lucien had not adopted Pierre? Would you have adopted a Jewish child, as
Lucien did, while living in Europe during World War II? Why do you think
as you do?

. . . .

. . . .

question 37

In the novel, Alain discovers what Lucien is doing. However, before he can tell anyone, Pierre kills Alain. How might the story be different if Pierre had not killed Alain? Do you think the story would be the same at all? Why do you think as you do?

. . . .

question 38

The author was an architect before becoming a writer. Would you have taken a similar path to becoming a writer? How do you think *The Paris Architect* would be different if the author had not had an architectural background?

Quiz Questions

. . . .

question39

The main character of the novel, _____, is a non-Jewish man living in France during World War II. He is approached by AugusteManet at the beginning of the story to help build hiding places for Jews.

. . . .

question40

_____ is a Jewish man living in France. He is hiding in AugusteManet's house. He wants to help other Jews escape from Europe by hiding them in similar places.

question41

In addition to working with AugusteManet and Mendel, Lucien also helps the
_____ by building munitions factories. However, he stops when he is
found out by the French Resistance.

question42

Lucien meets a woman named Bette, who is housing orphaned Jewish children. Lucien adopts one of the orphans, _____, who becomes the son he always wanted.

question 43

True or False: Lucien's opinion on the Jews changes after he discovers a Jewish couple has died in one of his hiding places.

question 44

True or False: Lucien's wife Celeste supports him in building munitions factories for the Jews.

. . . .

question 45

True or False: Lucien and his new family escape France at the end of the novel with the help of the Nazi, Major Herzog.

. . . .

question 46

The author of *The Paris Architect* is _____. He was born in Maryland in 1954.

question 47

The author studied _____ at the Pratt Institute. He later studied _____ at Columbia University.

. . . .

question 48

Before becoming a novelist, the author wrote in the _____
genre about architecture. He was inspired by _____ to
become a writer of fiction.

. . . .

question 49

True or False: The author used his experience as a hobbyist painter editing his paintings to edit his books.

question 50

True or False: The author is also a historic preservation specialist in addition to being an architect, painter, and novelist.

QuizAnswers

1.   Lucien
2.   Mendel Janusky
3.   Nazis
4.   Pierre
5.   True
6.   False, she is against him working with the Nazis.
7.   True
8.   Charles Belfoure
9.   Architecture; Real Estate Development
10.   Non-fiction; John Grisham
11.   True
12.   True

THE END

Want to promote your book group?
Register here.

PLEASE LEAVE US A FEEDBACK.

THANK YOU!

  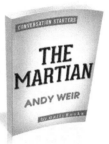

36163919R00039